Praise for *Prophets of Morning Light*

Love, loss, friendship, sexuality, familial relationships, the sensory Caribbean, political and artistic figures from Margaret Thatcher to Joan of Arc to Audre Lorde: Patricia Harkins-Pierre masterfully and with an exquisite luminosity explores all from a distinctly yin perspective of the human experience.

~ Mary Alexander, Founder of Rock Lounge: Open Mike Poetry, St. Thomas

Patricia Harkins Pierre's *Prophets of Morning Light* is as gorgeous and many-layered as the Caribbean life she celebrates—replete with colors and "strange airs" that recall the magical world of Shakespeare's sprite, Ariel. Patricia's mystic sense of uplifting sights and her terrifying glimpses of hidden darkness create their own *Tempest*, in storms of elation and passages of sorrow. These poems, more vivid than photographs or movies, resound with Caribbean rhythms, contexts, and extravagant leaps—even unto angels (who, very likely, are intimates of poetic spirits like Ariel). Patricia's poems vibrate with intimate grandeur. Enter here; be charmed by her perceptual fields of liquid blue outreaches, her stratospheres of disparate jewels.

~ Diane Sautter Cole, PH.D., Poet and Professor of English, Northern Michigan University, Marquette, Michigan

Light...and darkness...co-exist at the nexus of *Prophets of Morning Light*. Dr. Patricia Harkins-Pierre shares the poet's vantage without flinching, illuminating equally beheadings, butterflies and bougainvillea. Beauty abounds, seen through prisms of Southern light; but so does bitterness and bile. Love and loss lie as lovers in this little volume that is part memoir, part rite of passage, part essay, part scripture, part dark humor, part cautionary tale, part enlightened scream and all poetry. It's an intensely personal journey where fantasy, hope, heartache and reality dwell as one; and a journey I encourage you to take.

~ Dr. Doug Larche, Senior Fulbright Scholar, Author of *Truth on Trial, Angels in the Snow, Number the Stars*, and *Father Gander*.

Prophets
of
Morning Light

Patricia Harkins-Pierre

Negative Capability
PRESS
MOBILE, ALABAMA

ACKNOWLEDGEMENTS

Some of the poems in Prophets of Morning Light have appeared, in one form or another in the following journals, anthologies and collections: *Negative Capability, The Caribbean Writer, Seasoning for the Mortar, Island Poems, Akpasa, Tigers in Paradise* and *The World Record*.

DEDICATIONS

The author wishes to thank her husband for his loving patience, as well as Dr. Sue Walker, editor and publisher of Negative Capability Press, for her continuing encouragement and inspiration. Thank you as well to the amazing writers in my manuscript workshop group at the Mayapple Press Writers' Retreat, Woodstock, New York this summer (2013) who gave me such important insights as I revised and re-arranged the poems in *Prophets of Morning Light*. Finally, thank you to Judy Kerman, founder of Mayapple Press—dear friend and enduring mentor.

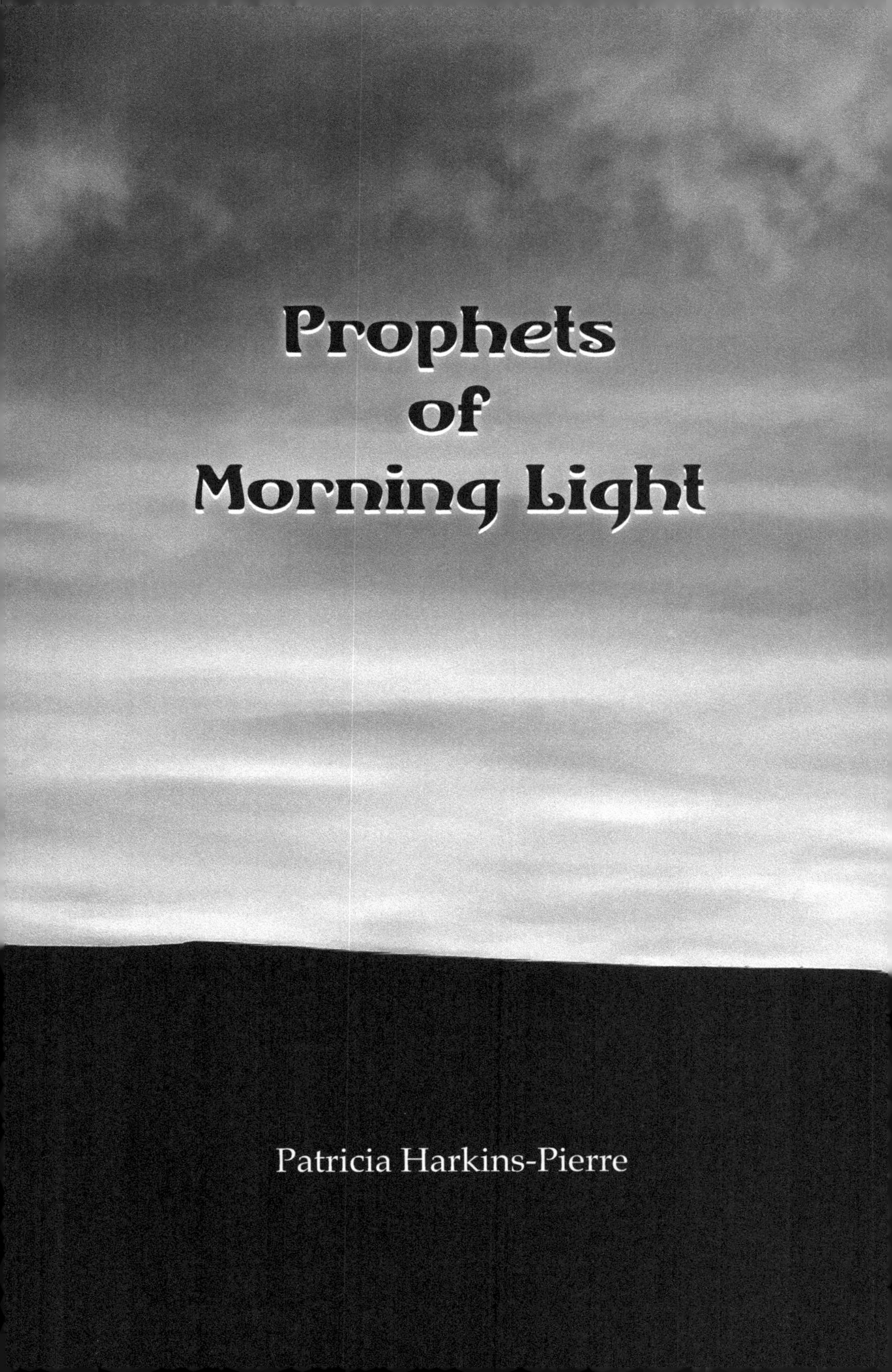

Prophets of Morning Light

Patricia Harkins-Pierre

A Negative Capability Press Book

Published in the United States of America by
Negative Capability Press
Mobile, Alabama

Editorial Assistant: Stephanie Feather
Cover & Interior Design by HTDesignS

Printed in the United States of America

ISBN 9780942544879
LCCN 2013954508

Scan to visit
www.negativecapabilitypress.org

Scan to visit and like
Negative Capability on Facebook

TABLE OF CONTENTS

Prophets
of
Morning Light

Church in Brittany

They walked the cliffs
on their honeymoon,
made love in the dark.

Home again,
she found herself alone.

Twenty years later,
on a difficult day,
she closed her eyes
and met him again.

Under her eyelids,
the church in Brittany,
stars on the ceiling,
a faded fresco on the wall:

the 'Dance of Death'
chanting,
He who sows
hope in the flesh
reaps bones.

Deep as the Caribbean Sea

My mother is made of glass.
She eats off of dishes so sharp
they cut her tongue. Years ago
my father stopped eating. He sits
on the porch in a wicker swing
and practices fishing.
Sometimes the silence between them
is clear and deep as the Caribbean Sea.

Telling Daddy

I was getting out of my car at the Seven-Eleven
the first time we met.
Willie took his sunglasses off to wink at me.
His eyes were two shades darker
than his skin. His hair shone more
than my patent leather shoes.
"Daddy, I love him," I said.

Six months later, after Sunday dinner
Mama twisted her wedding band.
"Nothing Gail does surprises me."
The Boston Celtics were on TV.
With two minutes left, the game
was tied. Mama turned the sound
off. She put her hand on Daddy's shoulder.
"Joe?" But he just sat
at the kitchen table
and wrote a check for a hundred dollars.
"Here," he told me.
"Spend it on yourself."

Locked Door

Together we inhabit one skin
while snow swirls on the TV
screen, behind clear, cold glass.
It's dark on the other side
of our locked door.
We are laughing. One
or both of us close to burning.
Turning away, letting go,
we drift.

After You Know Me

You were so quiet
the first time.
I felt like a puppy
licking your hand.
The sweat on your forehead
shimmered in the light
from the bamboo lamp.
Under your dark, lazy gaze
I wished for a patch
to hide behind.
You had entered my thoughts
through my body.
I couldn't be still.
You kissed my eyelids,
I said nothing,
wriggled away.
Rolled back.
"I'll never get used to you."
You smiled,
a little fold
under your eyes lifted. My
hands opened, relaxed.

Behind God's House

I gave myself away at twenty-one
and took a dead nun's name.
Mary Frances. In that disguise
I've taught the children
at St. Luke's for twenty years
to write their names, spell the months
and tell the time. Each day
I walk the halls in thick-soled shoes
that squeak. My rosary swings
against my thighs. God watches
from the window of his house next door.
He knows my chastity is technical.
I dream of skin—sleek and smooth.
Isaac, the gardener, barely knows me.
Digging in the dirt behind God's house,
he puts his open mouth against a flower.
It's June. The sun is hot.
Isaac's shirt is off. He gleams with sweat.
His smell is bitter. I'm cleaning weeds

from the graves of nuns and priests.

Honeymoon

Salt smell of semen,
bitter taste of perfume
as we wrestled
on the Paris hotel floor.
We never saw Notre Dame
that summer, 1965.

Walking the frozen woods,
behind my father's house
six months later
how cold the envelope felt, and thin.
I weighed it in my hands.

Your letter, mailed from Saigon,
arrived two weeks after
they wrote me
the jungle ate you alive.

I turned to mother, laughing.
"See, I knew Davis
could never die
so far from home."

Sunday Afternoon

On Sunday my husband takes his belt off
to use on me while football players
fill the screen in waves
of red and white, blue and gold.
The players and I rise and fall;
rise and fall. It's all we know to do,
until the half-time band begins,
then Carl is ready for beer.
He passes out before the game is over.
When it's time for the post-game show
I watch three cheerleaders stack themselves,
a sweaty pyramid for the cameramen.
After I turn them off, I brush my teeth
(brushing away the taste of blood). Shower, go to bed.
My mouth is sore but I smile in the dark,
inhaling the smells of peppermint and talc.

Collect

You phone me. Collect.

I should hang up.

It's almost midnight.

But you know the code.

"The first place we lived. On Catherine Street.

Apartment 3-A. Tell me."

I close my eyes, begin the story.

"We furnished the apartment with

ferns in brass pots,

twin porcelain cats with blue eyes.

We dragged our grandfather clock

up three flights of stairs before we fell

onto the patchwork quilt

from St. Ann's church bazaar."

It's your turn now.

"The first time I said I loved you

was when I proposed.

Next day we found those cats.

You still have them, right?"

I open my eyes. "Only one."

Song for My Daughter

Your eyes, blue,
with gold centers
like tiny suns,
will never startle anyone
but me. Like a French queen,
I am dressed in white
to signify mourning.
Yesterday I was fertile.
My husband laughed
when I put my red dress on.
"Silk? For the hospital?"
Last night my mother
sat with me, patting my hand.
"Al has kids already,"
she said. "And just think,
now your stomach will always
stay flat." I dreamed
I was a pear so ripe
my skin split open. Sweetness
poured from the wound.
When I woke up
my mouth was dry.

An egg the size of a pearl

lay exposed to the sun.

A stranger bent over me.

"Rest yourself, baby," she said.

"It's all over now."

Grandfather's Trousers

Grandmother starched my Grandfather's shirts:
white cuffs, pointed collars;
ironed his narrow-striped ties;
folded his sober socks like napkins;
even his hat had to stand at attention—
she dusted the brim with a turkey feather—
until, at noon, on her forty-fifth birthday,
after serving him lunch in his study,
she stripped his favorite dark blue trousers
off the ironing board in her kitchen,
ignoring their knife-sharp creases,
ignoring Grandfather's call,
and left.

Death-watch

Grandfather refused to die
on the clean white sheets
of a hospital bed.
He chose Mobile Bay,
night fishing last June.
After he fell, his boat
floated on the surface, an island.

Coast Guard divers hauled him up.
Two young men in uniform
put him in a green plastic bag.
"Like trash," Grandmother whispered.
Aloud she began, "Our father who art. . . "
Mother shook her head. "Don't pray for him.
He didn't really fall, you know. He dove."
Grandmother cried so hard she couldn't answer.
I watched the divers strip their frog feet off
and lift their masks.

Grandmother draped herself in black.
Mother wore navy blue, with pearls.
After they left in the limousine
I walked down the hill
to Grandfather's dock
and shied wet stones at his boathouse.

White Gloves

Grandmother wore white gloves when she smoked,
and hid her Kools in a jewelry box.
She had an amethyst ring set in silver
and a bracelet of gold and jade.
She played Mozart every night,
her fingers flashing across the keyboard.
Grandmother never baked cookies,
darned socks, or raked the backyard.
She combed my hair until it gleamed
and braided it into an auburn crown.
She tucked me in at night and pulled
the covers tight across my chest.
When I was sick, her fingers, cool and white,
massaged my forehead, back and neck.
Grandmother's eighty now, and dying.
Asleep on a hospital bed,
her blue-veined hands are morning-glories,
I only watch.

Grandmother's Saints

My grandmother lies
in the high white hospital bed
in her short white hospital gown
all winter long. She looks
like the porcelain doll she bought
at auction when I was nine.
I wind my grandmother's
hair around my fingers;
sing her a lullaby:
"Your daddy's a sailor —
your mother's a swan."
My grandmother's feet
are always cold. Her wrist
bones poke at her skin.
Her mouth hangs open.
When I lean close, her
sour breath assaults me.
"Becky!" she calls.
But my name is Beth.
"I'm here," I say.
She points to the ceiling
and talks to her saints.
Michael, Christopher, Theresa.

Sometimes I take her
eggshell skull between my hands
and press down, down,
whispering, "Grandmother,
do you know that I love you?"

Death by Fire

At first, the hospital room
was cold. Grandmamma
held my hand.
"Don't be afraid for him,"
she said. "He'll be glad to sleep.
That's all death is."

Then Grandpapa opened his eyes,
sat straight up.
"I'm wearing a shroud," he said.
I stared.
Grandmamma patted my back.
"He's out of his head. That's all."

Grandpapa threw his covers off.
"Somebody help me! I'm on fire!"
He beat the air.
Grandmamma was gone.

And I wrestled that old man I loved
to keep him still.
Locked him in a hug so tight
we grafted together.
"I'm Jacob," he cried.
"You must be Gabriel!"

At the funeral,
Grandmama's tears meant nothing.
Whenever she says he had a stroke,
I touch where my eyelashes used to be.

Driving Lesson

Grandmother wore flannel nightgowns
with plain white buttons
even in summer. I never asked
why. Her feet were so small
my five-year-old brother could wear
her high heels. We used to watch
her dress for church. Sometimes
she let us braid her hair.
She said, "I don't like children."
When I was ten, she taught me
to drive. "Close your eyes, Gran," I said.
"Pretend we're flying." She did.

Grandmother Stockbridge

The summer I learned to smoke
Kools and drink Jack Daniels
my grandmother found me
propped on my elbow, reading
a *Playgirl* magazine. "Gail?"
I squinted up, into the sun.
The hair on Grandmother's arms
caught fire. She stood still
in the light, burning, white
against gold. Three years later
she died. I dreamed I stole her
ashes and scattered them,
then watched her rise.

Aunt Janet's Legs

Aunt Janet's legs change color
every day. I walk behind her
up the stairs, watching how they move,
together-apart; narrow-wide,
like scissors flashing yellow,
crimson, peacock blue. She likes
short skirts that hug
and earrings big as moons.
Once I saw her,
after an August thunderstorm
stretched out like a starfish
on the wet lawn.
in sunlight her legs were white.

Cobwebs and Bones

We found her sleeping alone,

elbows angled like wings,

knees folded into her chest;

a single bone bracelet

circling her waist;

this girl, lost for thousands of years.

Her hair fell over her eyes

in tangles as soft

as owl feathers.

Her doeskin skirt was fringed with shells,

Her fingers, laced together,

her ankles crossed.

Exposed to the sun,

we knew she would crumple to cobwebs and bones.

So we wrapped her gently,

sealed her away in a box.

The local newspaper headlines read:

"Beauty Shrouded in Mystery."

Sometimes I see her in dreams,

running on strong brown legs.

For Kevin

Yesterday at five-twenty
while I waited for a light
at Airport Boulevard
to change to green,
you transformed yourself
from the living to the dead.
How did the gun barrel feel
against the skin at your temple?
Cold as the Idaho lake water
we dove into
when we were thirteen,
shivering as we touched
the slick bottom?
I see your blood.
When your wife found you
did she kneel by your head —
or stand and stare,
twisting her green jade ring,
then let you go?

A Catholic Solider Recalls Vietnam

Our helicopter crashes.
Sulphur of burning—
jungle and wood,
cloth and skin,
paper and hair.
Crossfire cuts Tom in two.
Men, like torches, flesh
smoking, scream. Two soldiers
are blown to pulp. And Tom —
without a head —
walks past me —
two steps, three, before
he falls. After that
I do dark things —
Kyrie Eleison; Christie Eleison;
disembowel a woman, a child;
march on, until
black smoke thickens
the quiet air, so much,
no one knows when night
begins. In the dark,
blood gloves my hands.

Mono no Aware: The Pathos of Things

I close my eyes, remember
two kimonos,

folded flowers, obis
lying beside them

the one on top
catches the sun

chrysanthemum gold,
through the open door—

Mother, her face
the mask of a snowy owl

the white timbre
of her voice.

Ting. Ting. Notes
of her samisen.

Tonight I will dream
of Mother in October

a pine-covered hill,
crickets in the grass,

our neglected family
garden, a stone

pagoda,
a faded red gate.

I bend to pick
a purple flower, heavy

between my fingers
drops of mist on the green sepals,

a sound of water I walk to
over crackling bamboo

through a spider web —
floating threads cling to my hands.

Kibi Tateishi Thinks of Koshin, Her Brother

Hiroshima, 1945

My hair drifts like dandelion silk,

wisp after wisp.

Through my fingers.

Burns blossom on my hands.

Our mother's skin

ravaged with roses,

our father's ashes

mixed with earth,

are my garden now.

You are the single living flower.

Forget your sister.

Skin, brittle as birch bark,

peels from my fingers, my palms.

The nurse tried to feed me

today through a glass tube.

I turned my face away.

Madi's Mask

I watched a black head roll
in burning dust
on a Biafran afternoon
when I was ten.
I watched bored soldiers
kick their toy
away from the body
that used to clothe my brother's soul.
I wanted to catch his head,
close his eyes,
sing his spirit to heaven
with grandmother's prayers.
But I was afraid
of Madi's blood.
I was afraid
of my dead brother
whose face was a grinning mask.

Sisters in Spirit

Indira Ghandi is dying.
No, she is already dead.
Margaret Thatcher waits
for official confirmation.
Indira's death
will not be mourned by everyone
either here, or in India,
a country at war with itself.

And Margaret Thatcher thinks of England.
She sometimes dreams
she's blown apart.

She remembers, how,
not long ago,
Indira was the woman waiting
to learn the truth,
Margaret the leader
who might be dead.

Imelda Marcos Becomes Invisible

It's midnight.
Imelda Marcos sits
at her dressing table.
This is the smile she'll give
the reporters tomorrow.
She dips her hand
in cold cream the color
of morning glories.
She wipes away the layers
of carmine, of turquoise. She
rests her elbows on her knees,
lets the Kleenex drop
to the carpet,
almost forgotten.
She raises her head
toward in the light,
pretending she's invisible.

The Color of Death

Sagbadjou sits on his green plastic throne
and dreams of his grandfather's kingdom,
his grandfather's wives. The old man doesn't watch
his own women. The youngest are hanging
garlands and beads below the photograph
of Lenin, on the scarlet and ocher walls
of the Thunder Pavilion. "The people's Republic
must be modern," they say. "No more ancestor
worship." They whisper behind their hands,
"Our husband is like a rotting tree."
They click their tongues as they pass.

Jijibou, the big-bellied prostitute
squats in the dust and fans the king, hoping
he'll pay her with Elephant Beer.

Sagbadjou shuts his eyes but still sees the walls
of the palace his grandfather, Geza built,
stained red from the 'birds' of his harem,
sacrificed to appease him in death.
The sight of blood always sickened Geza.
But war was for taking heads. His leopard wives
understood. They were warriors. He loved them

because they were virgins. They called him

"Dada." They learned to fire muskets

and scale palisades of prickly pear.

They filed their teeth to sharp points.

After battle, they offered him

warrior's skulls, women's skulls, children's skulls.

He slept with a basket of skulls

by his ivory headrest. "I'm alive

in the world of real things," he said.

Banishing Witches

It's my sixtieth birthday.
But when I dream
I am five years old—
there's a witch in my closet.
I wake up, sweating, missing my mother.
The cat in the window
comes when I call. We walk
through the house together.
Then sit on the back porch swing,
watch stars spin patterns of light. Her fur,
an electric cloud, crackles and sparks
under my hand. Her eyes
are moons without shadows.

Zebralight

You taught me the landscape of lust.

Geography lesson over,
the river bed is dry.

I study sin.
My eyelids conceal

the blackness of Egypt.
Three moons eclipse the sun.

When I wake up
Zebralight is falling like snow.

Tigers in Paradise

Look closely.
Walk softly.
Tigers are here
in paradise

They stride through tall grass,
glide over sand,
melt into dappled trees
golden.
Ebony.
Emerald eyed.

Or white alabaster
striped with black.
Sunshine and shadow.
Eyes amber.
Eyes wise.
Eyes wide as Caribbean skies.

Spillover

Imelda Marcos dreams
of three thousand pairs of shoes,
and machine guns, countless
as stars, spilling
out of her closets at home
across carpet green as moss,
and as soft to her bare feet
with their scarlet toenails.
The shoes have stiletto heels.
The machine guns gleam.
Imelda Marcos puts on
a pair of glass slippers
the color of hummingbirds' wings.
In her brown arms
she cradles steel. She is singing.
It is Ferdinand's birthday.
While he watches
from a rattan chair, perfect
in the white linen suit
she bought for him,
she throws back her head.
Diamond clips flash
in her midnight hair.
Without aiming, she fires.

South Acre Child

(in memoriam)

The London Times said:

"Margaret Elizabeth Fountaine,

elderly spinster, English woman,

respected lepidopterist,

collapsed on the island of Trinidad."

Her estate consisted of butterflies,

22,000 stored and ranked,

drawer after drawer, in mahogany cases.

"A beautiful, slightly chilling sight,"

Her biographer notes.

She also collected a million words

in twelve identical leather volumes

with red ink borders. Between the thick pages

her editors found flowers she'd pressed

as she passed through Turkey, Australia, Hungary.

Her last entry, in 1940, begins:

"To the reader, yet unborn, I leave this record."

Telling the Truth about Audre
(in memory of Audre Lorde)

"Across the marvelous arithmetics of distance. . ."

A black woman rises

from the ashes of a body

burnt by cancer.

"Heat rises like mist. . ."

from her skin,

a " sacred and different" invisible mantle

she wraps around

sisters like us

who are "stretching to muscled limit. . ."

impossible languages—Swahili, Hindi,

Mandarin, Dutch.

She reads our possible fates aloud:

"Afraid is a country with no exit visas."

But we too can choose to travel, as she has,

"Staking a claim in difficult places. . ."

We will cross borders at midnight, singing!

Sweet Flesh, Sharp Bones
(for Audre Lorde)

Two women in one skin:

I. Black and tall.
    See her stride
    on long, strong legs.
    A basket of words
    like ripe golden mangoes,
    balanced on one wide hip,
    against sweat-pearled
    sweet flesh.

II. Grinning with pain
    from fatal wounds.
    Honey-comb skull.
    Shoulder blades
    sharp as daggers.
    Pelvic arch
    a wide open door
    her son, her daughter
    knew better than lovers.
    Dry, delicate ankle bones.

Joan on Fire

One day, in my garden by the Meuse River,
Archangel Michael, gloriously winged,
appears to my Joan in a blaze of light.
"Be a good girl," he tells her, smiling.
"Great things are expected of you."
My Joanie is only twelve and small
for her age. "You can't mean me."
She runs off to feed the sheep.

Three times the same week
that archangel comes to call
surrounded by hosts of glittering angels
perched in our willow trees,
speaking in tongues of flickering fire.
Joanie stands still. Listening.
(She doesn't know I follow her.)

Then two queens of heaven,
with golden crowns, appear
by the edge of the forest
under the ancient beech tree,
smelling as sweet as crimson roses.

They surprise her. "Daughter of God,
Do you know who we are?"

("My precious girl," I want to protest.)
"St. Catherine! St. Margaret?" she answers.
She's heard their soft voices in dreams.
She falls to her knees, embraces their feet,
vows to die a virgin, like them.
A martyr. A saint.
(I'm too stunned to protest.)

For four long years she hears the same voices.
Rustling poplar leaves,
ringing church bells,
they counsel her:
"Live a pure life."
(And I approve.)

When she finally turns sixteen
I hope she'll marry
and settle down.
Forget the dreams and visions of childhood.
But her voices don't stop.
Instead they've changed—
gotten louder—demanding.
"Daughter of God,"
the saints ask now,
"Why do you wait?
The need is great.
Leave your village.
Go! Save France.

Joan doesn't answer.
Archangel Michael
delivers this charge:
Relieve the siege of Orleans.
Lead the Dauphin to Reims
to be crowned.
Drive the English
at last from French soil."
My Joanie weeps in sorrow and fear.

We're standing in the Wood of Oaks,
tall trees with strong hearts.
Later that day I speak to her uncle,
Durand Lassois, a man of faith.
The next morning, early, my innocent child
sets out from home, but not alone.
My brave girl, in her patched red dress
and broken shoes, her dark hair
modestly hidden. On fire for God.

That night my husband has a dream.
His daughter has run away with soldiers.
Bewildered and angry, he wakes at dawn.
"If that's where she's gone," he tells our sons,
I want you to drown her. If you refuse,
I'll drown her myself, with my own hands."
Too far away for us to see
Joan of Arc travels far from home.

The Care and Feeding of Tropical Angels

I'm learning the language my mother knew.
Beside my grandmother's gate on St. Croix
fruit bats swoop and glide
in the green twilight of trees,
over the black tar road.
White butterflies weave
through the grass. Flamboyant trees
turn the summer breeze scarlet.

In the cool white shade of her Danish house
my grandmother lives with angels, porcelain
dinner bells Grandfather brought from France.
Crimson wings fade to rose
in leather-bound missals.

Of seven sea-island sisters
she is the only one who refused
communion; never confessing
in St. Luke's church, on the corner of King Street and Tern.

At dusk, no one but me
sees her kneel by the star apple tree,
scattering crumbs from English wafers.

At midnight I see angels
Flock her lawn, pink flamingos
That take flight at dawn, the quicksilver
Pulse of wings, like laughter.
At breakfast, my grandmother smiles:
"¿Anoche, abri mis vetanas, y tu?"

(Last night I opened my windows, and you?)

Slippage

Head bowed,
the bearded lady sits alone.
Hands folded.
Strands of fine hair
float from her chin.
She's lost her mind,
at play in the meadows of morning,
chasing ribbons of light. . .
or out for lunch,
sampling Chinese buffet
on a cruise ship in Mexico,
falling in love again
in a language
that's spelled like it sounds. . .
or maybe—like me—she's lost
in an ocean of tears
that can't wash us clean:

Oh Mama, I'm calling your name
but you've forgotten who I am.

The Bearded Lady Speaks

The bearded lady speaks to me
in a language known only to God.
Her eyes, once blue topaz,
are clouded with unshed tears.
Confined to her metal chair,
her feet curled up like cats asleep,
she shakes with cold
in spite of the jacket I crocheted,
the knitted robe. I try
to warm her hands in mine.
"Mama do you know me?" I coax.
Her smile is a riddle I cannot solve.

The little man sits in a corner
nearby. I watch him
pretend to watch TV.
"My head if full of white cotton,"
he says, and turns to me,
yearning. "Do I know you?"
"Oh, Papa," I start to chide.
But he isn't wearing his hearing aid.
We stare at each other. Lost
without language. Always strangers.
Never friends.

Heavy Handed Man

Oh heavy handed, solitary soul,
as darkness turns to dawn your eyes, aswarm
with flies, will greet the rising sun, behold
the restless sea. But see no more. The warm
salt wind will still caress your skin. But you
will never speak of how its kiss can steal
away your breath without remorse. This new,
bright day is meaningless to you, who feel
no joy. How innocent of guile was that
young girl who haunted every dream; whose tears
you said you'd wash away like rain. The rats
could smell your sweat last night, your lonely fear.
Today they feast on fruit, and flesh and lies.
No child will bear witness. Only the flies.

a girl who was raped refuses comfort

she feels like a drowned cat –
that clawed the man
who hung a stone around her neck –
that hissed and spat as that man
dumped her into the dark bay.
she knows how the cat's ruffled fur
flattens against its spine,
how its mouth snaps shut
against dirty water
and understands what the cat sees –
heavy, rigid, soaked to the bone,
staring into the still cold.

After Rape, a Terrible Joy

After the rape,
joy like the tip of an angel's wing,
glimpsed at dawn,
seems to elude the boy
forever.
Twelve years old
he teaches himself
to walk on stilts
above the sounds
of accusing voices,
and disbelief.

No one can reach him
anymore. No one
sees his blood and tears.

At Mass one Sunday
an altar girl
dressed in white,
carries the cross.
When the young priest
smiles from the pulpit
only the boy sees

invisible flames
ten feet high
wrap her in pain.

Only the boy knows
he's discovered his twin.
Oh terrible joy.

Requiem for Gene

"Where are you going?"
I asked. Gene turned.
Slowly. In pain.
"Home, Patricia. I'm tired."
He walked away,
into the rain.

Three nights later,
his loss like bitter green fruit,
I close my eyes.

A man of many seasons
sits under a mango tree.
Rain drops on his hands,
seasoned with pepper sauce
and lime.

I cannot speak
or touch his hand.
"Where are you going"
I want to ask.
He turns. Smiles.
"I'm passing through

to realms of glory."

"I'm passing through," he says,
laughing. "Passing through
to the other side."

Sweet Letting Go: Approaching Fifty

To be absent from the body is to be present with the Lord (2 Cor. 5:8)

Death
by drowning
is sweet.
Not the
desperation;
the choking,
pain
that swells
burns
and fills
mouth,
lungs,
brain.
But the sweet,
slow
letting go.
The pulsing
crimson
visions
radiant,
with light.
Do you see me

slipping free,
leaving behind
jellyfish body,
staring eyes?
Watch while
I rise
from the grave water;
fly
through the brilliant sky!

Pumpkin Women, Impossible Men

Impossible men
grow on trees,
green fruit, ready to drop
into the laps of too-willing women
who stretch their hands out.

Impossible men
last for a season.
Too-willing women
walk barefoot at midnight,
hands empty,
bellies full
of bitter wind.

Pumpkin women,
older, wiser,
jump for joy
when their bellies are full.
Give birth at midnight
to words bursting
with seeds
like pomegranates.

Pumpkin Dreams

I look in the mirror —
See ginger hair streaked with grey,
hazel eyes webbed with lines,
stout hips, sturdy thighs.
I want to cry but instead
curl up with my cat. We nap.
Pumpkin dreams of backyard ponds.
Sun warm on her broad back,
she's fishing. She licks her paws,
anticipating a feast.

The Power of Bears

I see six bears dancing
under my willow tree.
Dipping their paws
into bowls of green Jell-O.
I stand on the back porch,
watching. When they lift their muzzles,
dripping with sweetness,
I take a step forward.
"I'm coming too.
Wait for me."
But the bear
with the silver collar,
the biggest bear,
turns away. And they go —
leaving their empty bowls behind,
upturned in the wet, still grass.

White Cat

The white cat stretches across the fence.
Her long tail spills like milk,
that, crouching, I catch in my hands.
How sweet it smells, and warm.
It tickles my nose. I bend it
into a fat moustache. My daughter
stands on tiptoes. "Gimme," she says.
With a single shrug of one white shoulder
the cat retreats up the willow tree.
From far below, we watch her tail
whip the trailing green leaves
as she rides the top branches into the wind.

Cloud of Witnesses

I. A cloud of green
    parrots, gregarious
    clowns, yellow
    chests bursting
    with laughter,
    race the blue breeze —

II. Deer step softly.
    Their delicate hoofs
    imprint the grass.
    Plump parrots rise
    in clouds of glory.
    Their raucous calls
    pierce quiet dreams.
    The morning light is clear.
    A white cat crosses the road
    in peace. No one sees
    hummingbirds feast
    on hibiscus blossoms,
    or two deer
    grazing on sweet green grass.

Comfort in Calamity

Beautiful are the feet

of those who bring good news

to deserts of doubt,

to islands of despair —

Who bring the hope

of comfort in calamity.

For them, beloved,

joy is a seamless coat

clothing dry bones,

woven of light.

Crowning Joys: For Glen

I long for a son
who follows his father
as day follows night;
a daughter
whose smile is the shadow
of all the hours I lost
gladly to hours
tasting like mangos and lime,
when only the moonlight clothed us;
when even the sunlight
was simply a halo to crown
our joy.

Love Feast: An Island Ode

Southern Whites fall
from the sky like snow
onto sorrel, cocoa plum,
passion fruit islands.

White butterflies
like migrating angels
pause in flight,
feast on mangoes,
and plantains sliced thin
as communion
wafers – on coconut
tarts – guava jelly:
On Montserrat pineapples
dripping with gold.

*Note: Southern Whites are type of butterfly common to the
Caribbean region.*

Test Match

"This is the tea break.
Stay tuned for live cricket."
The screen is blank
of brown skin,
pink skin,
white collars,
white pants
no longer immaculate.
Grass streaked,
dust streaked,
time and sun combine —
Stain even the captain's
scarlet hat with sweat.
In the stands one idle fan
swats flies.
Another, belly bare,
swigs beer.

The field is empty.
A single hawk hangs,
high in the flawless sky of Barbados —

Prophets of Morning Light

Daughters of God
Join hands – let us walk
On the water
In St. Thomas harbour

Let us dance
On the wide wings of pelicans
Floating beneath our feet
Like grey clouds
Yellow beaks full of fish.

Let us sing,
Prophets of morning light.
Yes! Let us speak life:
Benediction, Blessings,
Alleluia! Amen!

Wanda Under the Angel Tree

She doesn't see angels
anymore. But under the mango tree,
she does see Wulf.
He's wearing white,
immaculate, debonair.
He offers her three flowers,
hibiscus, bougainvillea, rose.
When she questions him,
he dries her tears with kisses,
dusting her open mouth with pollen
tasting of honey,
of ginger and rain.

Post Hurricane:
Open Letter to the Author of "Easter Wings"

Dear George:

Hurricane winds have passed

leaving me flat

laid low

as the mango tree across my lawn.

I used to dream about wings

but now I don't dream at all.

Night of Grief

You sin. I burn. This night of grief no light
will steal across the hot and dirty floor.
Without delight, we speak of love. In sight
of death your voice is cold. I watch the door
in hope of quick escape but finding none
resign myself to lies. The wind outside
is moaning like a woman wooed—then shunned.
I know her name. I see her face. I've tried
in vain to comfort her. Your words slice deep—
I hurl them back. Too slow. The bitter taste
of rust and bile is strong. I long to sleep—
to abdicate. Create. Inspire. Not waste
my tears. You lean away from me. I learn
a new, small word: despair. You lust. I yearn.

The Sovereign Spaces of Thought

(Caribbean Studies Association Conference: Nassau, Bahamas)

Ideas – bright blue flags unfurled

in rooms where flowers climb and leaves uncurl

in red, in green, in pink profusion,

in lovely, rich and lush confusion.

Pale carpets hush loud shoes, while curtains plush

as velvet, smooth as milk will smooth, not crush

our conversation. I watch sudden smiles

like signal lights flash on, flash off. Meanwhile

our hair, our eyes, our skins, our clothes shine

like jewels, electric gems. Desire to find

release of thoughts too long confined will spill

from sheets of brilliant black seed pearls; fill

the sovereign spaces of our minds; swirl

through blood and bone to permeate our worlds.

Sudden Joy

Wet grass—glass sharp green
smell slicing through early mist.
Wading knee deep in

sulphur butterflies.
Suddenly—hummingbird wings—
Early morning joy.

Christmas Angels in Paradise

I. St. Croix
Butterflies
drift down
sunlit streets
like sea island cotton:
It's white Christmas
in Christiansted.

II. St Thomas
Across the blue water
in Crown Bay harbor
cruise ships float
like tropical icebergs
tethered to concrete docks.

III. St. John
Cattle egrets
with wings white
as Christmas angels
feed in long grass
near Cruz Bay.

The Wings of Moths and Hummingbirds
(CW Humanities Prize 2007)

The wings of moths and hummingbirds invade

my dreams. Their feathers stroke me, soft as suede.

Awake, I watch for dawn, imagine love,

the wings of dragonflies and brooding doves,

of herons pure as light and parrots bright

as day, that rise to greet the sun. The sight

of sugarbirds with butter breasts, the sound

of thrushies bold but liquid voiced, I've found

illuminate my heart, inform my words

all day. I look for terns and gulls, those birds

whose wings cut sharp across the sky; who dive

with pelicans through salt rich sea. I thrive

when hawks with fierce brown gaze and soft gray breasts

lift up their wings to ride blue wind. I'm blessed.

www.ingramcontent.com/pod-product-compliance
Lightning Source LLC
LaVergne TN
LVHW091205080426
835509LV00006B/842